Back to the Old Days

WESTERNS

ROGER GEACH

Copyright Book Law Publications 2010

ISBN 978-1-907094-58-3

Bibliography and web pages

There are numerous web pages and books published on the Class from photographic albums to technical reviews.
The ones I have found most useful are listed below.

For the information on 'Western'-hauled rail tours during 1976/1977 and all other tours I recommend the Six Bells Junction website run by Gary Thornton at http://www.sixbellsjunction.co.uk

For information around Exeter and details of movements, Sean Greenslade's splendid information to be found on 'Exeter Rail Blast from the Past' at http://www.exeterrailways.co.uk

For detailed history of the 'Westerns' the following three books by Adrian Curtis have provided an invaluable guide: 'Cast of Thousands' (published by A&C Services, 2001, a bible on works visits, liveries and shed allocations), 'Western Liveries' (2001) and 'Western Mythology' (2003)

The following photographic albums:

'Western Diesels in Camera' by J. Vaughan (Ian Allan, 1977) 'The Heyday of the Westerns' by D. Huntriss (Ian Allan, 2003)
'The Westerns' by H.L. Ford and N. Preedy (Bradford Barton, 1976) 'The WR Diesel Hydraulics' by H. Dady (Ian Allan, 1989)
'The Power of the Westerns' by C. Judge (OPC, 1977) 'Diesels in Depth - Westerns' by D. Clarke and J. Jennison (Ian Allan, 2007)
I also consulted various Western Region Working Timetables

(***Front Cover Picture***) 1001 WESTERN PATHFINDER departs Bodmin Road with 1B11, the 08:30 Cardiff to Penzance on Whit Saturday 24 May 1975. Bodmin Road, situated in the Fowey Valley, was remote but acted as the railhead for large parts of North Cornwall following the closure of the Padstow and North Cornwall line. The town of Bodmin itself was about four miles away. The junction station (now renamed Bodmin Parkway) was always fairly busy. No.1001 was introduced to traffic on 12 February 1962 and was withdrawn prematurely on 4 October 1976 after being involved in a collision with a Transit van which had stalled on a crossing at Stoke Cannon, north of Exeter, during the early hours of the Sunday morning, 3 October 1976. The locomotive was working the 1B79, 23:15 Saturday night Paddington-Penzance newspaper train.

(***Back Cover Picture***) 1023 WESTERN FUSILIER departs Newton Abbot with the 15:30 Paddington to Penzance on Monday, 19 May 1975 at 18:54. No.1023 is in worn work-stained condition with the yellow front starting to fade and stripes appearing. It was not until September 1976 that the loco received a Laira repaint with silver buffers, and became the railtour engine along with 1013. FUSILIER was the last 'Western' overhauled at Swindon Works and spent from 10 August 1972 until 20 September 1973 in the works, well over a year. At one time there was doubt if it would ever be completed and for a period, work was stopped on the locomotive and it could have been the first taken out of traffic. As we now know this was not the case and the locomotive was also dual-braked at this time, the last one to be so fitted and emerged from the works on 13 September, only to return the next day for rectification repairs. On 23 September 1973, I admired the loco at Laira depot where she was gleaming in the sun; her new paintwork looked magnificent. The staff at Swindon had done a great job, the likes of which we were never to see again.

First published in the United Kingdom by
Book Law Publications 2010, 382 Carlton Hill, Nottingham, NG4 1JA
Printed and bound by The Amadeus Press, Cleckheaton, West Yorkshire

WESTERNS AT WORK

This is a photographic album which looks back at some of the services that the 'Westerns' worked. It does not offer a history of class, nor is it a technical publication. Others can write about the history, their performance and detail differences far better then I can.

It is a photographic record of the everyday scene as recorded at the time with particular emphasis on their 'home patch' of Cornwall and Devon. I make no apology for including a large number of pictures taken here as this is where fellow photographer Bernard Mills and I spent most of our time. Maybe I was in a field near Bolitho and he was at Berry Farm. We recorded the common scene as it was then. If the 'heavy showers' came and spoiled our fun one day we could always come back the following week and see the same trains.

Many of us tend to recall the 'Westerns' in blue as this is how the class was in the 1970s. No.1046, the last maroon 'Western', went into Swindon Works during February 1971 so, from then on, we only saw blue 'Westerns'. Many photographers did not record diesels during the mid to late 1960s as they were busy chasing the end of steam, so pictures of 'Westerns' at work during this time are not that common. This is particularly so throughout South Wales where the everyday scene is less well recorded compared to South Devon. I have endeavoured to find some unpublished pictures of maroon 'Westerns' at work during this period and these have all been taken in the south west. You can see that their maroon paintwork fared little better than blue for keeping its shine and weathered just as easily as the later livery.

Back down in the far west, as the 1970s went on things started to change as different types of locomotive appeared. First there were more Class 47s, then 'Peaks' and finally, from May 1974, the dreaded Class 50s. This all, of course, meant less 'Westerns'. I have not set out to include an example of each locomotive as certain engines are rare on film, especially the early withdrawals. The Landore air-braked 'Westerns' were scarce down west as they worked the Swansea to Paddington and Bristol services and rarely came off that route. The West Country drivers were not trained on air-braked passenger trains until later, around 1971. Our local Plymouth Laira 'Westerns' were far more common. No.1051 was top of the list having arrived at Laira during January 1964 and stayed there throughout its working life. In contrast, No.1066, the first dual-braked 'Western', was hardly ever seen during this period in the south west, spending all its time working from Landore. When looking back at my notes, none of the 'Westerns' were that rare in 1972, it's

just that the same ones seemed to get captured on film more than others. Of course, any in the works at Swindon would appear to be scarce as they were often out of traffic for a number of months. The vacuum-only 'Westerns' were particularly active that summer, often turning up on the Motorail service to St Austell or working china clay trips from St Blazey. Little did we know at the time they would be early candidates for withdrawal.

At the time of writing, it is more than 33 years since the last 'Westerns' were withdrawn. Studying the photographs from back then it is often apparent that the background scene has changed just as much as the motive power. Some stations, like Plymouth, do not appear to have changed that radically, but as for poor old Newton Abbot, well, enough said.

Remember the lines of telegraph poles that followed the Up side? Most of them went not long after the 'Westerns' in Cornwall, around 1980 as I recall. They were as much a nuisance to the photographers at the time as the Cornish drizzle, which ruined many a day's photography. The platelayers' huts were also found along the railway and these too have now all but disappeared. Embankments have become very overgrown, ruining once favourite locations - the Cornish showers and sunshine combining to ensure rapid growth of foliage.

The greatest change, however, is the traffic and rolling stock, both freight and passenger. The modern railway has few freight services now in the West Country with very limited block trains. All the wagons depicted here are long gone, just like the locomotives that hauled them. The milk, general freight, newspaper, perishables, parcels and mail traffic has all gone. With the loss of the freight traffic many station siding sites have now disappeared beneath car parks or have been built over to become supermarkets or industrial estates. Housing developments have also covered some locations and road improvements. For example, try finding Blagdens boat yard as depicted in the introduction.

Passenger stock is mundane comprising mostly HST and modern multiple units, often overcrowded due to the limited number of coaches. Locomotive hauled trains are now the exception rather than the rule. Most of the locations that do survive are also devoid of any rolling stock. Driving down the congested Embankment Road at Plymouth recently, as well as looking out for the speed camera, only one coach was seen stabled outside the once mighty Laira depot. It was never like that in the old days!

BACKGROUND

If you travelled on British Railways' former Western Region during the 1960s and up to 1977, the chances are at some point a 'Western' diesel-hydraulic locomotive would have been at the head of your train. The 'Westerns' were loud, noisy and at times, when pulling away, emitted an exhaust that put many steam locomotives to shame. They were very quick to accelerate away from station stops and could re-start trains on heavy gradients. Living down in the far west in rural Cornwall, they were in the mid-1960s, along with the 'Warships' and North British Class 22 locomotives, very active on the Cornish main line. It was not until the summer holidays of 1967 that we noticed something different when the Brush Type 4s, later Class 47, started to appear across the Tamar Bridge. These locomotives made a different noise and admitted a vertical plume of smoke when departing rather than the classic 'vee' of the hydraulics.

The hydraulic classes were deemed non-standard by the British Railways Board and they chose to get rid of them and concentrate the fleet on diesel-electric types. First to go back in 1967 were the five original North British 'Warships', all withdrawn at the end of the year. The 800 series 'Warships' were next and the run down continued. It was not until the autumn of 1971, when a massacre of 'Warships' and 'Hymeks' took place, that it really sank home to us that the hydraulics were disappearing fast.

From early summer 1971 we noted the sad sight of a long line of withdrawn 'Warships' shunted into Hackney Yard, east of Newton Abbot. Bristol Marsh Junction also started to fill up with redundant locomotives. At first the 'Westerns' remained untouched, but for how long? In those days news travelled slowly. What happened in January we would read about in the May issue of 'The Railway Magazine' or 'Railway World' if we were lucky!

Once the 'Warships' had all gone, by the end of December 1972, how long could the 'Westerns' last?

Local enthusiast Sean Greenslade had recorded detail movements through his home town of Exeter from 1969 and he was on hand at Taunton travelling back to Exeter St David's on Tuesday, 9 January 1973 when he rode behind 1032 WESTERN MARKSMAN heading west with the 09:30 Paddington to Penzance. Sean remarks in his notebook that this was a very poor engine when climbing uphill, though it still managed 96 mph downhill on that run! No.1032 departed Exeter and was never seen working a train again by any of the West Country boys.

We know through records that 1032 arrived at Laira depot, Plymouth, on 16 January around midday. The locomotive showed a flaw on one of the axles and a request was made for a replacement bogie but, due to the financial budget for bogie work being exceeded that year, repairs were refused. While other repairs were also required it was this decision that led to 1032 being sidelined and it never worked again. This was the start of the rundown of the class. No.1032's official withdrawal came on 6 May 1973 quite some time afterwards. It was not until that spring that many of us realized what

had happened as 'Westerns' started to appear on the dump. At first the locomotives were seen still with their nameplates on and, indeed, both 1061 and 1007 seen on the dump in April 1973, were returned back into traffic. No.1032 did not, neither did 1039. Quite when 1032 first appeared on the dump I do not know, it was certainly there by early April 1973. As we all now know, that was that and the dump started to fill up over the next four years with our beloved 'Westerns'.

I hope that you will enjoy this photographic journey from the capital to Penzance. This trip does wonder off-route at times to include coverage of some of the other lines that the 'Westerns' worked along with some diversions! For example, I am pleased to be able to include some rare pictures taken in South Wales during the 1970s.

In the early to mid-1970s a 'Western' almost always came around the corner - whether it was on a passenger train, milk tanks, clay hoods or vans - those were the days I recall the best and I have tried to illustrate them in this book. I have tried to show the ordinary everyday workings of the 'Westerns' as it used to be in more carefree days so the younger generation can see what we got excited about while the older enthusiasts can remind themselves as to how it used to be. In those days there was no high visibility clothing to contend with on the trackside. One could ask for and usually be granted lineside photographic permits and there was no security staff at stations. Some of the people who have contributed to this book worked on the 'old railway' and would have access to what is now forbidden territory. This was especially the case at depots where one could wander around safely without a second thought, permission to do so was almost always granted. Access was provided to the motive power, offices, signal boxes, stations and trackside. It was a very different world to the one we now live in.

I would like to thank, in no particular order, the following friends and colleagues for the use of their photographs and/or information in addition to their company in times past and present. The use of their work and information has enriched my photographs and memories. Photographs not credited are my own while all others by the named photographers. Some film has passed the test of time better than others. Film speed was much slower; I used mainly Kodak 25 ASA. Colour film was expensive in those days and was used sparingly. Again, it was a different world to today's digital photography.

Thanks to the following contributors: Tony Wardle, Bernard Mills, Tony Smith, Peter Bowyer, Greensheds, Stephen C. Marshall, Sean Greenslade, Robert Aston, Martin Street, Stephen Howard, Peter Crawley, Doug Nicholls, M. Casper, R. Stone, Ian Harrison, Neil Phillips, Ian McDonald, Adrain Curtis.

I would also like to thank David Allen of Book Law for supporting the idea for this book, David Brown for proof reading and checking the captions, plus all the people past and present who enjoyed a trip and yarn about the 'Westerns' and the railway they ran on.

1000 WESTERN ENTERPRISE is pictured at Plymouth station's Platform 8 waiting to depart with 1A75, 16:20 Plymouth to Paddington on Sunday, 25 March 1973. From January 1968 until October 1971, No.1000 was a South Wales locomotive and based at Landore depot, Swansea. Consequently the locomotive was rather less common down in the West Country. However, I recall seeing the rather scruffy 1000 at Plymouth during a summer holiday trip, providing a rare sighting of the loco in the South-West in 1970. From October 1971 the locomotive, along with all the others, became Plymouth based. However, no sooner had this allocation taken place than the locomotive was called to Swindon Works for overhaul, so it was not until April 1972 that we saw the locomotive return with its nice clean coat of paint along with newly fitted air brakes. You could tell this engine apart from all others by the much deeper nameplates. No.1000 was never a particularly common class member and met a sudden end when, on 6 February 1974, it was working a special 08:00 Tavistock Junction ballast train and collided with a 'Brute' parcels trolley at St Austell station. The collision caused damage to the buffer beams and frames which was enough to warrant withdrawal rather than repairs. The locomotive was cut up quite quickly at Swindon works, but the nameplates survive, one set at the National Railway Museum and one set at Swindon Steam Museum.

This is the view from the Embankment Road bridge by Laira depot looking towards Tavistock Junction, seen here in late September 1970. A scruffy Crewe-built, blue vacuum brake only 'Western' is heading 1C55, the 12:30 Paddington to Penzance, due Plymouth at 16:30, and is seen passing a fine bracket signal by the Plym estuary. On the left can be seen Blagden's boat yard fed from an inlet beneath the railway. This view was to change radically from 1973 when the A374 road was widened and a dual carriageway built above the former boat yard. At the same time the manual signalling was replaced by colour-light signals. The signal boxes at Mount Gold and Laira Junction were decommissioned from 11 November 1973. **Photo B. Mills**

This is the present view as seen on the 7th April 2010 from the Embankment road bridge almost in the same spot as Bernard Mills was some 40 years earlier to record the 1230 Paddington to Penzance service. The only main line certificated Western to run on the National Railway is the Diesel Traction groups 1015 Western Champion which is pictured working the 1Z52 Bristol Temple Meads to Plymouth leg of The Great Briton Rail tour. One wonders how many of the motorists filling up at the Texaco filling station would know that once this was the corner of Blagden's Boat yard and was a far more tranquil scene then the busy road that it is today. Bernard was also on hand to witness a Western once again passing the Plym estuary and we were able to reminisce about the past.

The gateway to the West for many was London's Paddington terminus. Enthusiasts departing from here would hope for a 'Western' for their journey west. This view from the country end of Paddington station on the morning of Thursday, 9 May 1974 shows that anyone travelling on the 09:30 departure that morning was in luck. No.1011 WESTERN THUNDERER is seen waiting to back onto the coaching stock to form the 09:30, 1B25 Paddington to Penzance. Earlier, 1011 had brought the empty coaching stock into Paddington to form the 08:30 service to Paignton, and waits in the sunshine. The locomotive is in weather worn condition with a typical side-swipe gash under the nameplate. A number of other 'Westerns' also ran in service with this type of damage over the years. A visit to Swindon Works for overhaul saw these war wounds removed. The 09:30 from Paddington was regularly 'Western' hauled, with Class 47s also appearing on this service at times. Following the timetable change from Monday, 6 May 1974, Class 50s started to work services to the West as well. No.1011 received a much needed repaint during October 1974 at Plymouth Laira depot and subsequently looked much smarter that autumn.

The main depot for Paddington was Old Oak Common where the hydraulics could be found receiving maintenance, or stabled between duties, especially at weekends. Ranelagh Bridge just outside Paddington provided fuel and limited stabling facilities, but was used for the quick turn-round of locomotives working into Paddington. Seen at Old Oak Common on 8 November 1969 is Brush Type 2 No.5528, used on local coaching duties and brought in to replace the NBL Class 22s, such as 6328, which is also pictured here. Nos.1055 WESTERN ADVOCATE and 1060 WESTERN DOMINION stand around the turntable along with 'Hymek' No.7045 and another 'Western'. **Photo P. Crawley**

A different view of Reading General station as seen from the Western Tower offices of the Reading division headquarters, which overlooked the station, with the staff canteen giving a wonderful panoramic view. The 1A38, 11:20 Swansea to Paddington has arrived early at 14:15, due to call 14:17 to 14:20, with 1060 WESTERN DOMINION providing the power on a March afternoon in 1969. Behind can be seen the 3A48, 11:33 Paddington to Didcot parcels, formed with a DMU trailer and parcel unit complete with a white roof. This service was due at Reading from 14:23 to 14:45 and made a very leisurely journey from London to Didcot. A Class 33 can also be glimpsed, stabled between duties. The Motorail terminal sign informs customers that they could travel with their car to the West of England, West Wales and Ireland. The station totem signs are also still in place on the lamp posts, but there is only one car to be seen in this photograph. **Photo D. Nicholls**

1001 WESTERN PATHFINDER is seen heading 1V04, the 08:50 Birkenhead Woodside to Paddington express near Hatton during September 1962. The locomotive is depicted in as-built livery with a yellow buffer beam and coach maroon, no yellow panel. This engine was new on 12 February 1962 and received a half yellow panel from October 1962. Monday, 10 September 1962 was the first day of full diesel working on the Paddington to Wolverhampton services via Birmingham Snow Hill, 'Westerns' had started crew training well before that with 1000 itself based at Oxley from June 1962 and some services were 'Western' hauled from 25 June 1962. It was during this early period that 'Westerns' regularly worked the London to Chester route via Wolverhampton, Shrewsbury and Wrexham until Brush Type 4s replaced them during 1964, when the routes north of Birmingham were taken over by the London Midland Region. Later in the 1970s, 'Westerns' once again returned to work London to Birmingham services via Banbury, but this time to New Street rather than Snow Hill. So, the period of operation during their early days working as far north as Chester was quite short. It was a fascinating time but most enthusiasts were mainly interested in steam, so details of the workings are not so well documented as later in their lives. **Photo Greensheds**

1040 WESTERN QUEEN is already looking rather work worn and stained as it approaches' Hatton station with the 1A70 09.50 Aberystwyth – Paddington the up Cambrian Coast Express on a winters day during February 1963.

1040 was new to traffic from Crewe on the 20th September 1962 and was first allocated to Old Oak Common. The yellow buffer beam paint was extended over the lip as seen in this picture. The locomotive ran in this livery until it received a call to Swindon works during June 63 when it received yellow panels. This western was the first of the class to be involved in a serious collision at Knowle and Dorridge on the 15 August 1963 when it ran into a freight train conveying land rovers. The leading cab was badly damaged and a long works visit saw this cab renewed completely. The new cab end did not have headboard clips when the loco finally emerged from Swindon works on the 24 February 1964. **Photo Greensheds**

1064 WESTERN REGENT heads the 10:25 Birmingham New Street to Paddington away from Lapworth, near Solihull, on the morning of 7 February 1975. This locomotive had worked from Paddington that morning on the 06:45 departure and was returning as diagrammed. No.1064 was not dual-braked until May 1972 when released from its final overhaul at Swindon Works. Had 1064 not been involved in a minor collision at Plymouth Laira depot with 1046, then it may well have lasted right to the end rather than being withdrawn on 11 December 1975. **Photo B.Mills**

1016 WESTERN GLADIATOR runs round its train at Birmingham New Street having arrived with 1M11, the 09:05 Paddington to Birmingham on Monday, 15 September 1975. The return working was 1V38, 12:25 Birmingham to Paddington. No.1016 has the headcode wound up ready for that working. 'Westerns' were not regular visitors to Birmingham New Street until later in the 1970s when they started working regularly from Paddington to New Street and back via Banbury and Tyseley. Visits via Cheltenham and the Lickey on cross country services were quite rare, but did happen on occasions. When new from 1962, the 'Westerns' were booked on Paddington-Birkenhead services as far as Chester, but they would have visited Snow Hill not New Street.

On the lovely summer evening of Saturday 6, June 1970 at 19:20, 1035 WESTERN YEOMAN is seen arriving at Newbury with 1C72, the 18:30 Paddington to Plymouth, comprised of 12 coaches. Picture taken, the photographer then made a quick dash over the footbridge and caught this train home to Plymouth. The locomotive is looking quite clean as it had been overhauled, fitted with air brakes and painted from maroon to blue at Swindon Works, emerging in mid-February 1970. No.1035 had worked up earlier that day from Plymouth to Paddington on the 10:50 from Penzance and had a relatively quick turn-round at Paddington. **Photo B. Mills**

1012 WESTERN FIREBRAND arrives at Westbury station with the 1B15, 08:30 Paddington to Paignton on a lovely autumn morning of Tuesday, 16 September 1975. No.1012 was one of the five 'Westerns' fitted with an experimental ventilation vent to try and improve the flow of air into the cab to reduce the heat in the cabs during the summertime. Others fitted with this experiment were: 1028/1039/1056 and 1071. When this photograph was taken, No.1012 had only another six weeks left in traffic before being withdrawn on 2 November 1975.

1034 WESTERN DRAGOON enters Westbury station from the north on an empty set of PGA wagons on Thursday, 10 September 1974 at 15:59 passing a fine display of signals. While the headcode shows 8M07, this is incorrect as 1034 has been tripping between Westbury and the quarry at Merehead for most of the day. Westbury signal box was replaced by a modern power box which was commissioned from the 14th May 1984.

1055 WESTERN ADVOCATE approaches Fairwood Junction, Westbury, with 6V55 stone empties for Merehead quarry on Monday, 6 May 1974 at 14:29, formed of vacuum braked wagons from Westbury. Passing this service is 46051 with a loaded service from Merehead quarry. This train is made up of PGA wagons of which the front six have covers over them. The wooden platelayers' hut was cursed by photographers at this location as it could get in the way of your pictures. Other locomotives noted working stone trains around Westbury that day were: 1022, 1048 & 1056, along with Class 47s Nos.47122 & 47097, 'Peak' 46051 and Class 33 No.33005.

A classic early evening view from Bristol Temple Meads station looking towards Bath Road depot. A very work-worn 1019 WESTERN CHALLENGER is seen coming off shed on a fine evening, 8 September 1971. This locomotive had the longest nameplates of any 'Western' and, along with 1017/1018 and 1020, was never air-braked. These locomotives became prime candidates for early withdrawal, with their parts being used to keep others going, cannibalisation as it became known. No.1019 was called to Swindon Works for its final overhaul and arrived on 10 December 1971, emerging on the 17 March 1972. The locomotive was taken out of traffic on 2 May 1973, the first of the vacuum-braked engines to be stopped. It was quickly officially withdrawn on May 6, along with 1032. On the far right-hand side of this shot can be seen the tower which overlooked the dumping ground at St Phillips Marsh, where many 'Warships'/'Hymeks' and D63xx hydraulics were stored prior to scrapping at Swindon Works. **Photo P. Crawley**

1028 WESTERN HUSSAR heads north towards Bruton, Somerset, with 1A52, 11:25 Kingswear to Paddington on a very warm 12 August 1965. No.1028 was one of a batch of five locomotives, 1025-1029, built at Swindon without headboard clips. It was new to traffic February 1964, but you can see that the paintwork on the locomotive was already beginning to wear with some of the undercoat showing through. The first vehicle behind the locomotive is an ex-GWR Hawksworth brake third. **Photo T.Smith**

1035 WESTERN YEOMAN, working 1C75, 12:30 Paddington to Penzance, is seen just west of Bruton, Somerset, on 12 August 1965. This locomotive is seen in the green livery as worn by only seven members of the class: 1002 /3 /4/35/36/37 and 38. By early 1967 green livery was no more. No.1035 lost its green livery when it entered Swindon Works on the 3 November 1965, re-appearing during early February 1966 in maroon with small yellow panels. **Photo T. Smith**

1011 WESTERN THUNDERER stands at Taunton on Sunday, 3 November 1974 with the 08:45 Paddington to Plymouth. This service was routed via Swindon and Bristol Temple Meads to Plymouth and was a regular 'Western' diagram. No.1011 had been repainted at Laira depot emerging from the shed on 13th October 1974, so the paintwork was still quite clean. Part of the beading around the nameplate is missing and a number of 'Westerns' ran like this as a result of damage. No.1011 was to run until 2 October 1975, when it was taken out of traffic.

1010 WESTERN CAMPAIGNER is hauled away from Exeter St David's by an unidentified 'Warship' on Saturday, 14 August 1966. Note that 1010 has three oil lamps on the rear. The locomotive displays 1A42 in the headcode panel, which at that time was the 10:25 Kingswear-Paddington, so perhaps it had failed that morning. **Photo B.Mills**

1056 WESTERN SULTAN stands under the signal gantry at the west end of Exeter St David's station on Saturday, 11 May 1974, the first summer Saturday of the new timetable with the 1B55 12:30 Paddington to Paignton. This train was late as 1065 had arrived at Westbury from Paddington on one engine and had to be taken off. No.1056 had been hastily acquired off Westbury shed and took over this service, departing from Westbury at 14:40. Note the wrong headcode on the front of the locomotive, 8M53, which was a stone train working from Westbury. A group of young enthusiasts congregate on the platform end planning the next move or perhaps just observing what was passing through. Adidas bags were all the rage then, now these youngsters will now be around 50 years old! The start of the summer timetable that week had seen the introduction of booked work for the Class 50s. Out of sight on the stabling point were the following engines: 46011, 1028, 7016 , 47330 and 50003. The infamous 50003 was known to the locals as 'Policeman Plod' as it plodded along. On this occasion 'Plod' was a failure having been towed into Exeter the previous night by 47226 on the 15:30 Paddington to Penzance, having shut down near Heywood Road, Westbury. Some 106 minutes later things were moving again, just what you want on a busy Friday. 'Policeman Plod' was to fail many times before the fault was rectified and of the first batch of Class 50s to arrive this was, without doubt, the worst of the lot.

1044 WESTERN DUCHESS stands at Exeter St David's on 1B55, 12:30 Paddington to Paignton on Good Friday, 12 April 1974. At this time most of the main Down services would use this platform. A centre road allowed non-stop passenger services and freight to pass by without hindering passenger work. Exeter St David's was a very busy station and where the Southern line services from Waterloo terminated. There were also local services serving the Exmouth and Barnstaple branches, together with the stopping trains calling at the intermediate stations to Newton Abbot and Paignton. The re-signalling during the 1980s completely changed the platform workings at Exeter St David's. Today this platform is used mainly for Waterloo services. No.1044 did not work another summer and was withdrawn from traffic on 1 February 1975 as a result of collision damage.

1009 WESTERN INVADER at Exeter St David's on a winter timetable Saturday 6th April 1968 afternoon finds this clean maroon 'Western' waiting time with the 1V93, 08:50 Liverpool to Plymouth. Booked to stand at Exeter St David's from 14:52 to 14:55, this train then had a leisurely journey to Plymouth.

Photo D. Nicholls

On a lovely July 1966 Sunday summer evening, just after 19:00, an unidentified dirty maroon 'Western' passes Dawlish Warren with 1A98, 15:20 Penzance to Paddington. The siding on the right holds the camping coaches which have been situated at Dawlish Warren for many years. As can be seen, the maroon livery did not wear any better than the blue livery that replaced it. The Western Region washing plants and the chemicals that were used appear to have damaged the paintwork whatever the colour. **Photo B. Mills**

On a perfect May evening in 1969, a scruffy No.1009 WESTERN INVADER heads into Dawlish station with a London-bound service. The train is crossing Colonnade viaduct, the shortest viaduct on the Great Western. Even the contemporary cars by the viaduct would be collectors' items today. **Photo B. Mills**

1013 WESTERN RANGER on 1A79, 14:40 Penzance to Paddington, approaches a deserted Dawlish sea front on Tuesday, 20 May 1975 at 17:35. The sea wall and surrounds at Dawlish must have been the most popular spot for railway photographers in the country with countless visiting the area as well as the locals. One had to move around with the sun - if it was out! Up trains from the Newton Abbot direction were almost out of the sun at around 14:00 so not easy to photograph. I liked the sea wall and spent many hours there but it was better light in the spring or autumn, particularly for a before breakfast shot with the tide in and the sun out and a 'Western'!

The classic shot coming off the sea wall at Eastcliff, approaching Teignmouth. Generations of railway enthusiasts have observed movements along the sea wall. Here on a proper summer day, 1008 WESTERN HARRIER passes the holidaymakers with 1C55, the 1230 Paddington to Penzance on 23 July 1969. The tide is in and the sun is out, just about as good as it gets. No.1008 was one of the 'Westerns' that carried the maroon, full yellow front livery variation and ran like this from March 1968 until the end of June 1970, when called to Swindon Works for overhaul and dual-braking. **Photo B.Mills**

Here is a 'horror' picture that might upset some 'Western' enthusiasts, as Class 47 No.47171 hauls 1035 and 1003 away from Plymouth Laira towards Swindon, seen at Coryton Cove, Dawlish. This move ended up at Bristol Bath Road on this particular day, Wednesday, 21 May 1975. Such moves were rarely photographed as they were slow speed and quite often moved overnight. This was the only such move I ever saw in broad daylight, pictured at 10:52, and was pathed between the morning Plymouth Friary to Exeter Riverside freight and the 1M85, 07:40 Penzance to Liverpool. No doubt it spent some time in the loops that morning! No.1003 had been stopped since 16 September 1974 and 1035 since 28 December 1974, and had been cannibalised at Laira for spares used to keep other Class 52s in traffic.

An unidentified maroon 'Western' at Newton Abbot with 1C40, 09:30 Paddington to Penzance on a Summer Saturday during 1967. This was the period when many trains ran with a combination of maroon and blue/grey stock. The sidings alongside the depot also hold a rake of mixed stock. This depot was the home of the Newton Abbot allocated Swindon-built 'Warships' which provided power for the Exeter to Waterloo service until October 1971. The station appears little changed since the steam era with some attractive BR(W) chocolate & cream platform signs and station nameboards. The railway scene has changed so dramatically at this location. Today Newton Abbot has only three platforms. The motive power depot is but a memory, the sidings gone and industrial units built where once 'Warships' and Westerns stood on shed. An extended car park has been built over where the Up main and through lines once ran. **Photo D. Nicholls**

1065 WESTERN CONSORT stands in the early morning sun at Newton Abbot on Thursday, 25 July 1974 with 1A29, 05:05 Penzance to Paddington, 'The Golden Hind'. No.1065 had departed Plymouth at 07:00 having taken over from 1043, which had brought the portion up from Cornwall. The first class coaches and restaurant car had been added at Plymouth. This train was a popular service for business travellers to London from Plymouth, Torbay, Exeter and Taunton. Several of the local MPs would use this service from their constituencies to Westminster. They were none to happy when Class 50 No.50050 failed north of Exeter when working this train later in 1975 and they all missed a debate in the house as the 50's brakes were locked hard on. After that incident, double-headed 50s worked the train for a period after questions were asked in the house! Soon it was back to a single 'Western' as Laira preferred and trusted the 'Westerns' over a 50. No.1065 was one of the locos that did not have headboard clips at the 'A' end. It is seen in rather weathered blue livery and got in a much shabbier and work-stained condition during the hot summer of 1976.

1042 WESTERN PRINCESS is recorded at speed heading through Totnes station with the 1C51, 10:30 Paddington to Penzance, the Down 'Cornish Riviera' express on a summer Saturday in July 1967. At this time the train was timed to pass Totnes at 13:59. The coaching stock is made up of nine coaches, a mix of maroon and blue/grey Mk.1 vacuum braked stock which was typical of the period. Totnes was formerly the junction station for the Ashburton branch. Part of this line survives today as preserved South Devon Railway, but only extends as far as Buckfastleigh. The remainder of the branch was largely buried beneath the improved A38 trunk road. Totnes remains the railhead for the South Hams district of South Devon and is still quite busy. The water column is seen still standing opposite the signal box, which is now a cafe. On occasions in 2010, 'Western' photographer Bernard Mills could be found in the Booking Office selling tickets, or perhaps out on the platform watching the trains going by, though not often 'Western' hauled. **Photo D. Nicholls**

1030 WESTERN MUSKETEER passes Tavistock Junction working 1C55, 12:30 Paddington to Penzance during May 1968. This picture was taken from Lord Morley's bridge, itself now superseded by the A38 Plympton bypass. To the left is the recently lifted course of the double curve around to Marsh Mills, the start of the Tavistock branch. On the extreme left is the original South Devon Railway signal box of 1874 which, since this shot was taken, was sadly demolished before preservation of such important buildings was recognised. Tavistock Junction yard appears very full with wagonload traffic on this day. No.1030 was the first 'Western' painted in any shade of blue, back on 2 August 1966. The locomotive appeared in chromatic blue with small yellow ends with red buffer beams as seen in the photograph. The locomotive remained in this livery until it was called to Swindon Works for overhaul and dual-braking, entering the works during December 1969, being out-shopped in April 1970 and was then re-allocated to Landore depot, Swansea. **Photo B.Mills**

Home of the 'Westerns'- the classic view from the ramp after walking through the double doors from the train crew signing-on point into the main repair shed at Laira depot (LA), Plymouth, seen here on Sunday, 7 April 1974. No.1008 WESTERN HARRIER (on the right) stands next to 1025 WESTERN GUARDSMAN. No.1008 was in the process of receiving a repaint and 'C' exam, while 1025 was undergoing a 'B' exam. Other 'Westerns' in the main shed that day were 1071/1061/1029 and 1001. The latter locomotive was released and worked the 17:30 Plymouth to Paddington. All the 'Westerns' were based at Laira from October 1971 until the final day of the class on 27 February 1977. It was a short period of time that all 74 were in traffic and working from LA as 1032 was stopped for repairs on 16 January 1973 and never worked again.

It was Boxing Day, 26 December 1974, but in those days the trains were running. This picture shows the old steam shed side of Laira depot, which was known to us locals as 'The Dump'. It was here that the locomotives waiting parts for any length of time were stabled or the stored and condemned locomotives were held. No.1003 WESTERN PIONEER is seen on the stop block end of a driving car unit with 1008/1029 and 'Hymek' 7089 behind them. Also on 'The Dump' that day were Nos.1031/1045 and 1066. No.1003 displays the headcode '0F77', the running code for a light locomotive to Plymouth Laira depot. PIONEER still has its number and nameplates intact as the locomotive was not officially withdrawn until 5 January 1975. However, 1003 had arrived at LA depot on 16 September 1974, but was never to work again.

Sunday evening, 8 August 1976 and the train crew chat on the platform at Plymouth North Road at 18:40 after the arrival of the Up milk train, the 16:40 St Erth to Acton with super power 1071 WESTERN RENOWN piloting Class 47 No.47070. The modern office block - now known as Inter City House - opened by Dr Beeching in March 1962, dominates the scene behind the train and is a local landmark. This also provided local photographer and railwayman Bernard Mills a great place to photograph the trains from, especially when he was at work in the former Telegraph Office situated on the fourth floor.

1064 WESTERN REGENT has arrived at Plymouth station, or North Road as we knew it, with the 08:45 Paddington to Plymouth on Sunday, 22 December 1974 at 14:23. No.1064 looks quite smart having been repainted at Laira depot during September 1974. The low winter sun highlights the yellow front on 1064. This was the Sunday before Christmas 1974 and the station was busy with additional services running. Following 1064 into Plymouth was 1053 on the 10:20 Paddington to Penzance relief.

1034 WESTERN DRAGOON heads 1A48, 10:15 Penzance to Paddington, 'The Cornish Riviera Limited', off Weston Mill viaduct, just to the west of Keyham, during September 1968. At this time the viaduct was reduced to a single track while engineers replaced the decking, in addition to shot blasting and repainting the metal sides. Note the two Engineering Department coaches stabled beyond the train. At this time a pair of 'Warships' was booked to work this train from Penzance, but as can be seen a single 'Western' was substituted at times. Just to the left of 1034 is the rail access to Devonport Dockyard which still is in place today. On the hill beyond, the estate at Barne Barton is clearly visible. The railway line to the MoD at Bull Point, which served the Royal Navy, runs through the trees below the estate and had a daily freight working. **Photo B. Mills**

The Tamar road bridge opened in October 1961 and provided a nice new location to photograph the trains. It was a bit late for the steam era but little had changed in the era of maroon 'Westerns' with the double track of the former London & South Western main line from Waterloo, now the overgrown and single track Gunnislake branch prominent and passing beneath. On a July evening during 1968, 1035 WESTERN YEOMAN heads west with the 17:10 Plymouth to Penzance stopper. The semaphore signals and Royal Albert Bridge signal box stand out in the evening sun. These survived until Plymouth panel took over in July 1973. The car park by the Tamar Bridge holds some contemporary cars, no doubt some of the motorists are viewing the 'Western' heading west over Brunel's great bridge. Today the view from this car park is still magnificent on a clear evening, but sadly few trains of any interest or variety now pass by. **Photo B.Mills**

1025 WESTERN GUARDSMAN waits in the Up sidings at Liskeard with a special ballast train, the 07:30 Tavistock Junction–Liskeard, which had stone originating from Stoneycombe sidings. Stoneycombe was situated to the west of Newton Abbot on the climb to Dainton and provided train loads of stone for the railway's Engineering Department. Class 46 No.46004 passes with the 7S38, 10:10 St Blazey to Glasgow freight at 10:42 on Wednesday, 20 February 1974. The Class 46 worked as far as Exeter Riverside then returned west to Truro with the 14:00 freight from Riverside. This was a regular diagram at this time which could produce any Type 4 traction that worked in the west. The train crew on 1025 are waiting for a gap in the timetable on the Up line, which will not be until after the 12:25 departure from Liskeard. They will then work in section between Liskeard and St Germans dropping ballast as directed by the Civil Engineering staff. Such workings were common place in those days. Stoneycombe ceased to send out ballast by rail many years ago, while the sidings where 1025 stands have also been consigned to history.

1070 WESTERN GAUNTLET also known as 'The Glove' arrives at Liskeard just before the sun goes down with the Down 'Cornish Riviera', 11:30 Paddington to Penzance at 15:34 on Saturday, 8 November 1975, passing the signal box and the fine bracket signal on the Up road. This signal is still in place 34 years later, but the starting signal ahead on the Up road has been replaced by a colour-light. Signalled on the Up is the 14:00 Penzance to Birmingham, which was hauled by 1023 as far as Plymouth with 46017 forward. Liskeard station booking office buildings have been rebuilt in the 21st Century, but the Up-side shelters are still in place while the Down-side buildings were ripped down many years ago. Despite this Liskeard has kept its character and just occasionally you can see a 'Western' pass through on a charter train.

1045 WESTERN VISCOUNT waits time at Liskeard with 1B15, 10:30 Paddington to Penzance on Sunday, 1 September 1974. No.1045 had worked forward from Plymouth replacing 50039, which had worked from Paddington. On Sundays most down services changed locomotives at Plymouth. The fuel capacity was beyond most locomotives to work from Paddington to Penzance and return. Note the galvanised oilman's lamp hut just to the left. Huts and small buildings like this could be found all over the railway in those days but most have subsequently been demolished. No.1045 had an experimental windscreen wiper that was hung from the bottom rather than the top of the screen. This locomotive was, in my opinion, one of the best of the 'Westerns' and whenever I rode behind 1045 it went like a rocket with extremely fast acceleration and, with the right driver, unbeatable. However, 1045 did not last into December 1974, being withdrawn due to poor and corroded wiring. I last saw 1045 on Laira depot on Sunday, 8 December 1974 outside the daily shed looking in a sorry state and never to run again.

A bright sunny morning at Liskeard and the first northbound service of the morning on Sundays in those days was the 10:05 1A35 Penzance to Paddington. Seen at Liskeard at 11:50, No.1057 WESTERN CHIEFTAIN pilots 50046, working in tandem with a driver in each locomotive. No.1057 had worked west on the 6B09 milk empties and No.50046 on the overnight 1B83 23:45 Paddington to Penzance service that morning. Double heading in Cornwall was virtually a daily sight in the 1970s. This was to balance locomotives or return failures to Laira depot at Plymouth. One could see any combination of locos over a period of months. The most common double-headed train was the 1M74, 14:00 Penzance to Birmingham on weekdays. No.1057 was known locally by the 'Western' enthusiasts as 'Heinz Beans' due to the '57 varieties' reference in the Heinz advert. No.1057 has a faded front yellow end and a face had been drawn in the dirt. No.1057 was never repainted.

Moorswater Viaduct in the sunlight. 1033 WESTERN TROOPER heads the 1B83, 15:30 Paddington to Penzance service over the viaduct in the superb evening light on Saturday, 13 July 1974. The sun was not around far enough to illuminate the arches until well after 18:30, so this view with the sun out was very much a high summer picture. The trouble was that there was only one booked Down train in Cornwall where the desired picture could be taken in those days and this was the 1B83, 1530 Paddington to Penzance, due off Liskeard at 19:53. Many times I tried to get the required picture, but the sun would go in or it would turn very hazy or even worse a Class 47 would appear. Just occasionally things went right and this day had been a day of sunny spells and cloud. The sun had broken through the cloud at about half past seven so I waited, hoping the train would not be late. It was, but the sun was still out and at 20:07 the picture was taken. Despite trying this shot countless times this was the only decent shot I ever got in the evening with a 'Western' on the viaduct and the cloud behind. Dull, cloudy pictures were not the same.

WESTERN GLADIATOR heads 1A35, 10:05 Penzance to Paddington near Dobwalls on Sunday, 21 September 1975 at 11:39 on a day of sunny spells. No.1016 was a popular locomotive with the enthusiasts and was known as 'Gladice'. The name Dobwalls will mean to many the place where they stood in traffic queues when heading west on the A38. It was not until December 2008 that the Dobwalls bypass finally opened. The bodywork is in a typical worn state as 1016 had been repainted at Laira during April 1973, the last works overhaul being way back in July 1970, when the loco was dual-braked and repainted from maroon with full yellow ends. The depot washing plants and chemicals used in the 1960s and 1970s did not seem to do the paintwork any good and the undercoat and primer would soon start to show through as seen in this photograph.

After 20:00 on a lovely summer evening, 1036 WESTERN EMPEROR is pictured on the single line near Largan with 1B83, 15:30 Paddington to Penzance on Saturday, 28 June 1975.This section of line was singled in 1964 to help with the maintenance over the viaducts at St Pinnock and Largan. Largan signal box was situated in the isolated woods overlooking the rural wooded Fowey Valley, close to the well known Trago Mills discount store. From Bodmin Road to Doublebois it was an uphill climb and on a still Cornish evening one could hear the hydraulics working hard. Today it is the sound of road traffic you hear on the A38 beneath the railway.

1071 WESTERN RENOWN arrives at Bodmin Road at 11:40 on the 25 Feb 1975 with the 4B08, 10:50 Plymouth to Penzance vans which had followed, from Plymouth, No.46046 on the 08:00 Bristol to Penzance service. On the Up side there is mail and perishables to load onto the next arrival the 'Up Cornishman', 10:25 Penzance to Leeds, which that morning was worked by 1067. The daffodils are in full bloom and this was a lovely early spring day with unbroken sunshine. No.1071 looks rather the worse for wear with the weathered yellow front. This was put right in May when Laira depot repainted the locomotive. The experimental cab vent above the headcode panel can be clearly seen in this photograph.

1033 WESTERN TROOPER passes through Bodmin Road at 11:08 with an extra clay tripper from Tavistock Junction to Lostwithiel with clay for export. It is springtime and the daffodil bulbs are out on this fine morning Tuesday, 25 February 1975. No.1033 had already worked a set of empty wagons from Fowey to Tavistock Junction that morning, some three hours earlier. This was not the only 'Western' working on clay as 1052 was also working trips on the Fowey branch that day, while 1059 was on the 10:10 St Blazey to Exeter Riverside freight. A rake of van fits are to be seen in the back platform at Bodmin Road, having returned from Wadebridge that morning and awaiting onward movement back to St Blazey. One of the local Class 25s will arrive and trip them back.

Summer Saturdays bring back memories of hot sunny days and extra services taking holidaymakers to the West. While the weather was not always as pleasant as this, 1011 WESTER THUNDERER is pictured working 1B39, 10:56 Paddington to Penzance on the approach to Brownqueen Tunnel, which is near the local beauty spot of Respryn Bridge on the River Fowey. This was a very hot Whit Saturday, 24 May 1975. The 10:56 departure from Paddington was a timetabled service that ran only on a summer Saturday and provided a relief to the 11:30 Paddington–Penzance 'Cornish Riviera'.

Mention freight in Cornwall in the 1970s and one would think right away of china clay and milk traffic. In this picture we are reminded of both. Lostwithiel on a summer evening, Monday, 5 July 1976 and it is busy. No.1033 has passed with the 6M55, 18:05 St Blazey to Stoke on Trent clay and, just ten minutes behind, we see 1009 WESTERN INVADER arriving with the 6A21, 16:40 St Erth to Acton milk ready to collect some more milk tanks from the creamery. The driver is looking back waiting the shunter's instructions. Out of sight, 1051 has just departed with the 17:45 Plymouth to Penzance local passenger, while 25080 is waiting on the Fowey branch with a set of empty clay hoods for 1009 to depart to vacate the Up loop. The Down loop holds another rake of clay hoods. This is how it was in those happy days. The traditional clay 'hood' wagons are long gone, having been replaced by air-braked CDA wagons. The milk traffic has finished by rail along with most of the creameries they served.

Just before 11:00 on a very hot Wednesday, 4 August 1976   1065 WESTERN CONSORT is pictured on the Fowey branch near Milltown returning from Carne Point, Fowey, with clay empties. The Fowey branch was very rural and followed the River Fowey along its length from Lostwithiel to the jetties at Carne Point. This scenic line once had a passenger service, which was withdrawn as long ago as 2 January 1965. This locomotive was notable for its poor external condition when running in the summer of 1976, and there are numerous patches on the locomotive.

49

1009 WESTERN INVADER passes under the minor road bridge at Treesmill and climbs up towards Treverran Tunnel with the early running 7E19, 19:40 St Blazey to Temple Mills freight on the fine spring evening of Wednesday, 12 May 1976. This was one of the trunk trains that departed Cornwall in the evening conveying wagon load traffic, which would call next at Tavistock Junction, Plymouth. From 1 January 1976 the use of headcodes on the front of locomotives was abolished and many 'Westerns' had the headcode blinds wound up to display their number as seen on 1009.

1005 WESTERN VENTURER waits at Par Station with 1B81, 08:00 Bristol Temple Meads to Penzance. The locomotive displays the wrong headcode on the front, 7B33 which was the 14:00 Exeter Riverside to Truro freight service. They tended to be a bit slack with some of the reporting numbers down west and this day was obviously no exception. I recorded the train running slightly late so perhaps 1005 had been summoned to replace an ailing locomotive en-route that morning. One could always tell the 08:00 Bristol to Penzance as it had the buffet car marshaled right behind the locomotive. In those days it was the only train to convey a buffet in Cornwall. This was very welcome in the winter months as one could get a cuppa and sit in the front coach and, with the windows open, listen to the locomotive working hard up front.

A busy scene on 23 April 1968 by Par Bridge in the heart of the clay country. The first of the 'Warships' 800 SIR BRIAN ROBERTSON waits by the signal for permission to proceed towards St Blazey Yard with clay empties from Fowey, which has traversed the now closed route via Pinnock Tunnel and Par Beach. Par Bridge signal box can be seen under the viaduct with St Blazey shed beyond. In the foreground is the freight line that leads into Par Docks which still sees some sporadic traffic. Meanwhile, on the viaduct above, 1020 WESTERN HERO heads a morning Penzance to Paddington service towards Par station. No.800 did not last in service much longer as the locomotive was stored during September 1968 never to work again. The Par to Fowey mineral line shut from 6 October 1968 and work started immediately to convert the railway line into a private roadway for English China Clays lorry's to access Fowey Docks . A deal was done whereby all clay export by rail to Fowey was then routed via Lostwithiel to a much improved export jetty at Carne Point. Worthy of note is the single cyclist on the road towards Par Green - a very different view would be seen today as an endless passage of cars and trucks head by this location. **Photo B.Mills**

1065 WESTERN CONSORT approaches St Austell with clay empties from Carne Point, Fowey to Burngullow at 11:54 on Friday, 10 May 1974. This was one of the many clay trips that ran back in those days based on St Blazey Yard, and a set of empties would regularly be sent to load at Burngullow. On this occasion the empties were left and a different loaded set passed St Austell at 12:20 en-route back to Fowey. This was in the days when the 'hoods' first started to appear and only the very first wagon is one of the new modified 'hood' wagons. The tracks on the left led into the goods yard at St Austell which would take deliveries of household coal and other commodities brought in by rail. This has been closed for many years now and a housing estate stands on the old goods yard site. The signal on the right is for the Up road, sighted on the opposite side for better visibility and was clear for No.50027 on the 11:00 Penzance to Paddington which passed one minute later.

1021 WESTERN CAVALIER arrives at Truro with the 14:45 Penzance to Paddington perishables on Thursday, 23 January 1975 at 15:53 in the final stages of daylight. The train has just left Highertown Tunnel with the Malabar Estate visible above the train. This service conveyed a great variety of vans including the 'Siphon G' which can be seen in the consists third and fifth vehicles. There were 4-wheeled vehicles as well as bogie vans along with a composite brake which conveyed seating accommodation. On the right can be seen the warehouses built on the site of the former locomotive sheds and stabling area. Behind the train is the UKF fertiliser depot which received trainloads of products right into the 1990s. Truro once had a sizable goods yard which was re-laid and officially opened on 7 November 1971.

A view taken from the Up platform at the Plymouth end of Truro station during September 1968 with an unidentified maroon 'Western' on 1M05, 12:50 Penzance to Crewe perishables. At this time it was a Truro depot driver's turn from Penzance to Truro and on this occasion it was running early, booked to stand at Truro from 14:25 to 14:40. Behind is 'Warship' No.831 MONARCH on the 3A64, 13:12 St Erth to Acton milk, booked off Truro at 14:20. A couple of brake vans complete the view. Today most of the site of the former freight yard at Truro is a car park with only a couple of sidings remaining and very little freight traffic moves through West Cornwall at all. **Photo D.Nicholls**

No.1042 WESTERN PRINCESS arrives at Camborne with 1C55, the 12:30 Paddington to Penzance on Monday, 18 August 1969. Camborne served the mining area of West Cornwall and on the other side of the level crossing was situated the works of Holman Brothers, mining equipment manufacturers. Holmans was Camborne's, and indeed Cornwall's, largest manufacturer of industrial equipment including compressors and rock drills. The locomotive is in well-worn maroon livery with bits of paint missing from the front end beneath the driver's windscreen. It would be another ten months before this locomotive was called to Swindon Works for overhaul and to have dual brakes fitted, plus a coat of new blue paint. This was one of the early withdrawals being taken out of traffic on 18 April 1973. When this photograph was taken the signal box at the end of the Up platform and the old semaphore signals were still in use, but not for much longer as they were to be replaced from 8 June 1970 with Roskear Junction signal box taking over control of the section. The wooden crossing gates were replaced by lifting barriers, now fitted with CCTV cameras **Photo B. Mills**

1058 WESTERN NOBLEMAN approaches Hayle station with the 5E14, 12:20 Ponsandane to Plymouth empty coaching stock service on Sunday, 7 September 1975. At Plymouth the stock will form the 15:00 Plymouth to York service. This was one way the coaching stock was balanced from extra summer Saturday workings. This particular empty coaching stock train ran for only one season in summer 1975. The Hayle Wharves branch can be seen heading off on the right of the picture. Hayle box was switched out on a Sunday, with the signals pulled off the section would be thus from Roskear to St Erth.

1064 WESTERN REGENT has just shunted some vans and empty milk tanks into the down sidings at St Erth on Tuesday, 7 May 1974 at 11:40. Next No.1064 will depart for Dalcoath Sidings north of Camborne with more empty milk tanks and shunt them into the sidings there before heading for Drump Lane goods yard at Redruth. St Erth still is the junction station for the St Ives branch. There was also a small yard and a milk factory, part of which can be just glimpsed on the left. In those days the Milk Marketing Board controlled the distribution of milk. Standing in the yard are a number of the glass-lined milk tankers a very common sight in Cornwall until their demise in the 1980s. One is labelled with the St Ivel branding. While they appeared dirty on the outside, the tankers were glass-lined and the milk was pumped in and transported to the London area overnight. They were not refrigerated in any way. Every night of the week a train departed from St Erth at 16:40 with milk to Acton in West London. During the spring and autumn a second relief service ran, normally for six to eight weeks, departing at 13:50. No.1064 displays the headcode 6B09 on the front panel which was the 13:40 Acton to St Erth milk empties. This train made a very slow journey to the west dropping off milk tanks and shunting en-route departing Plymouth at 03:10 and reaching St Erth when it got there depending how much shunting was required on the way in the Duchy. The locomotive then spent the rest of the morning and afternoon tripping around West Cornwall as required before working a mid- afternoon freight back towards Exeter. All this freight traffic has been lost and the milk factory has closed. No milk trains have run in the West Country since the early 1980s.

No.1006 WESTERN STALWART nears journey's end with 1V70, 07:06 Bradford Exchange to Penzance, 'The Cornishman', at Marazion Marsh in August 1969. This service was timed to arrive at Penzance at 17:15 on a weekday and 17:50 on a summer Saturday. This view shows that fresh ballast had recently been laid on the Down road. This picture is taken from the coastal road bridge that leads from Long Rock towards Marazion town. After passing under this road bridge a wonderful view of Mounts Bay and St Michaels Mount would be visible to the passengers on this train. The railway followed Mounts Bay until the line terminated by the sea at Penzance. Marazion once had a railway station of its own but this closed to passengers on 5 October 1964 with freight facilities withdrawn on 6 December 1965. Many travellers will, like me, best remember Marazion for the old Pullman camping coaches that were located by the station site. The Western Region had an allocation of six newly converted Pullman cars as camping coaches in 1963; originally two were placed at Fowey and four at Marazion, but the following year they were all located at Marazion and used for Western Region Staff Association holidays in the 1960s and 1970s. Two coaches were removed for restoration and now provide accommodation at Petworth Old Station, West Sussex. Others remained at Marazion and became sadly neglected, victims of vandalism and arson attacks. Meanwhile, the former derelict station building has been restored and made into a dwelling. **Photo D.Nicholls**

1048 WESTERN LADY is pictured stabled on Long Rock shed at Penzance on the cold but sunny morning of Sunday, 9 February 1975. Behind the engine is one of the depot fuel tanks and a couple of open wagons. Long Rock depot is situated about a mile from Penzance station with Mounts Bay opposite, close to the passing main line and seashore. On a Sunday morning before the first trains departed the depot would be full of locomotives and this was a good time to make a visit. Also noted on shed with 1048 were: 1036/50007/47026/45003/50005/1041. At the station was 1065 and 50014 together with 47152, which had worked the overnight 23:45 Paddington service into Penzance.

1016 WESTERN GLADIATOR arrives at Penzance at 11:10 with 2C20, 07:10 from Exeter during August 1970. No.1016 had been overhauled and dual-braked at Swindon and released for traffic during July 1970. In the background can be seen the Hotel Royale overlooking Mounts Bay. Points of interest include the yellow destination boards seen on the Mk.1 coaches behind. The footpath along the wall seen above the coaches provided a wonderful view of the station and the bay beyond.

Saturday morning on September 4, 1976 finds 1068 WESTERN RELIANCE departing from Penryn with the 08:22 Truro-Falmouth formed of six air-braked Mark 2 coaches. A number of enthusiasts can be seen hanging out the windows listening to the sound of RELIANCE storming away. On arrival at Falmouth this train will then form the 09:10 departure to Paddington. This view from the footbridge is no longer possible as the bridge has been enclosed. The Truro to Falmouth branch has recently seen an investment programme with a passing loop provided at Penryn from May 2009, so that a half-hourly service could be run on the route. Back in 1976 some contemporary road vehicles are noted in the station car park and an industrial unit stands in part of the former goods yard site. The original station building was still standing when this photograph was taken but is set well back from the platform, being partially visible above the roof of the industrial unit. **Photo B.Mills**

One of the highlights of the summer Saturday timetable in 1976 was the introduction of the 09:10 through train from Falmouth to Paddington, offering the prospect of a locomotive-hauled passenger train on a branch line which normally only saw DMU operation. On Saturday, 18 September 1976, No.1041 WESTERN PRINCE is seen crossing Ponsanooth Viaduct, the fourth highest in Cornwall, at the head of the 09:10 Falmouth-Paddington. No.1041 worked this train to Plymouth and then worked back into Cornwall immediately taking over the 07:30 Paddington to Penzance service. In total the train was hauled by a 'Western' on seven occasions that summer with No.1022 being the last on the 25 September. No.1022 was also the only 'Western' to work the through service twice. However, it was not until 17 July 1976 that a 'Western' appeared on this service as the diagram was for a Class 50 off the 03:00 Plymouth to Penzance 'Brute' vans. However, enthusiasts were desperate to sample a 'Western' on the branch and words were had in the right ears and arrangements made so that, on 17 July, No.1072 worked the 03:00 Plymouth vans to Penzance, the 08:22 Truro to Falmouth and then became the first 'Western' to work the 09:10 from Falmouth to Paddington as far as Plymouth. **Photo B.Mills**

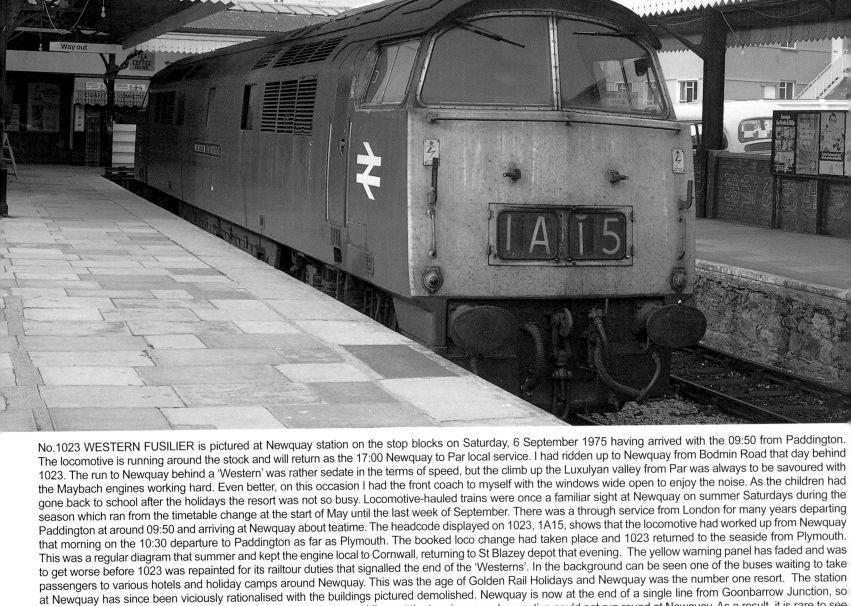

No.1023 WESTERN FUSILIER is pictured at Newquay station on the stop blocks on Saturday, 6 September 1975 having arrived with the 09:50 from Paddington. The locomotive is running around the stock and will return as the 17:00 Newquay to Par local service. I had ridden up to Newquay from Bodmin Road that day behind 1023. The run to Newquay behind a 'Western' was rather sedate in the terms of speed, but the climb up the Luxulyan valley from Par was always to be savoured with the Maybach engines working hard. Even better, on this occasion I had the front coach to myself with the windows wide open to enjoy the noise. As the children had gone back to school after the holidays the resort was not so busy. Locomotive-hauled trains were once a familiar sight at Newquay on summer Saturdays during the season which ran from the timetable change at the start of May until the last week of September. There was a through service from London for many years departing Paddington at around 09:50 and arriving at Newquay about teatime. The headcode displayed on 1023, 1A15, shows that the locomotive had worked up from Newquay that morning on the 10:30 departure to Paddington as far as Plymouth. The booked loco change had taken place and 1023 returned to the seaside from Plymouth. This was a regular diagram that summer and kept the engine local to Cornwall, returning to St Blazey depot that evening. The yellow warning panel has faded and was to get worse before 1023 was repainted for its railtour duties that signalled the end of the 'Westerns'. In the background can be seen one of the buses waiting to take passengers to various hotels and holiday camps around Newquay. This was the age of Golden Rail Holidays and Newquay was the number one resort. The station at Newquay has since been viciously rationalised with the buildings pictured demolished. Newquay is now at the end of a single line from Goonbarrow Junction, so only one train at a time can work in section. There are no loops or sidings at the terminus so a locomotive could not run round at Newquay. As a result, it is rare to see a locomotive-hauled train there today and any that do appear have to be 'top & tailed' with an engine at each end. Such is progress.

'Westerns' were only very occasional visitors over the former London & South Western Railway's Plymouth to Exeter line and very rarely photographed on this route except when they appeared on stone trains between Meldon Quarry and Exeter. What a joy it is, therefore, to find a picture of a dirty, maroon-liveried 'Western heading the diverted 1A57, 10:00 Penzance to Paddington 'Cornish Riviera' over the picturesque creek at Tamerton Foliot, Plymouth, just after 12:30 on a autumn October afternoon in 1967. This location still sees branch line services between Plymouth and Gunnislake, but unfortunately the alternative through route between Plymouth and Exeter closed in May 1968. This route followed the Tamar valley up through Bere Alston and onwards to the Stannary town of Tavistock before heading along the moors through Brentor and onwards to Lydford and Okehampton. On this occasion the 'Cornish Riviera', along with a few other services, was diverted due to a freight train derailment on the Dawlish route. The alternate route came in very useful when things went wrong or the tide washed away part of the seawall and track at Dawlish as tends to happen on occasions. No.1046 is thought to have been the last 'Western' to visit this section of line when it worked a demolition train away from Tavistock North on 14 January 1970. 'Warships' were the more common motive power on this section of line after dieselisation, being booked to work the Plymouth-Brighton through service and return. All booked locomotive-hauled services were withdrawn from this route from 6 March 1967, after which only DMUs were then used until the line was closed. The former L&SWR main line did have one weekend of glory before closure when, due to bridgeworks, the Dawlish route was closed and all main line services were diverted over the weekend of 21 October 1967 via Lydford. Many people in the west believe this line should never have been closed depriving the busy town of Tavistock of its railway. Despite campaigns to bring the railway back to Tavistock, it has yet to happen. **Photo B.Mills**

No.1021 WESTERN CAVALIER, working 1B29, 12:30 Paddington-Plymouth which had been diverted due to engineering work on the Taunton to Exeter line, is pictured on the old Southern route approaching Crewkerne Tunnel on Easter Sunday, 14 April 1974. This view shows how attractive the Somerset countryside looks in spring. 'Westerns' were not seen that often on the Exeter to Salisbury route, which at this time normally saw passenger services worked by Class 33 locomotives. On the odd occasions that diversions did take place, a real variety of motive power could be seen. **Photo T. Wardle**

No.1027 WESTERN LANCER stands at Kidderminster on Sunday, 28 March 1971, having arrived at 12:39, some 18 minutes early with the Plymouth Railway Circle and Great Western Society special, which had originated from Plymouth at 07:10. The route taken from Cheltenham was via Honeybourne and the west to north curve to take the tour onward via the Vale of Evesham to Worcester and Kidderminster, where a fleet of nine road coaches was waiting to take the West Country enthusiasts to visit the Severn Valley Railway. Unfortunately, on the return leg, No.1027, once the holder of the Paddington to Plymouth speed record, did not show her record breaking capabilities and was only running on one engine. The 'Western' was removed at Bristol with Brush Type 4 No.1912 replacing 1027 for the return to Plymouth, where the tour arrived back at 23:02, 17 minutes late. **Photo B.Mills**

Holgate Bridge, York, provided an unusual backdrop for a 'Western' on Saturday, 20 November 1976, as a gleaming 1023 WESTERN FUSILIER, complete with silver buffers, arrives with the Western Locomotive Association's 'Western Talisman' charter from King's Cross. This was probably the most unusual of all the BR era 'Western' railtours as it took a member of the class completely off its region onto the Eastern and the East Coast Main Line for a one-off special. The locomotive was fitted with the two black dot headcodes as this was an Eastern Region requirement at that time. No.1023 was the only 'Western' fitted with this modification. FUSILIER was repainted at Laira during the last week of September 1976 ready for its railtour duties. The first tour it worked wearing its new coat of paint was on 2 October 1976, 'The Merchant Venturer' from Paddington to Hereford via Newport in association with 6000 KING GEORGE V. Prior to its repaint FUSILIER had been rather scruffy. By a strange coincidence, No.1023 was to take up residency in York, as part of the National Collection at the National Railway Museum. Photo **T.Smith**

No.1052 WESTERN VICEROY stands at Derby on Saturday, 29 March 1975 with the Plymouth Railway Circle and Wirral Railway joint 'Western Sunset' tour. The locomotive had worked forward from Westbury to Derby taking over from 1036, which had brought the train from Plymouth departing at 07:15 via Honiton and Yeovil. This tour was the last charter to traverse the direct line from Cheltenham to Stratford on Avon via Honeybourne before the line closed. 'Westerns' had worked to Derby occasionally on passenger services in the past. During the summer of 1971, the 09:40 Saturdays only Bristol Temple Meads-Derby and the return 13:23 Derby-Paignton service was booked for a 'Western', but did not always get one. One particularly memorable occasion was when Derby Works held an open day and 1061 turned up on this working, much to the pleasant surprise of many. No.1060 put in an appearance on 26 June and 1020 on 7 August. This offered the rare opportunity to sample a 'Western' north of Birmingham. Cross Country relief services also saw 'Westerns' occasionally reach Derby, for example No.1029 worked a 10:12 Penzance to Derby relief on 20 December 1973. 'Westerns' often got taken off these services at places such as Bristol or Gloucester and trains were re-engined. Certainly if you managed to find a 'Western' on a West Country relief heading north you were lucky if you got to Birmingham with it still on. On every occasion I rode on one of these trains, the 'Western' was removed, usually at Bristol. **Photo B.Mills**

On a lovely sunny afternoon, Friday, 25 July 1969, No.1034 WESTERN DRAGOON departs from Cardiff with 1F43, the 14:00 Paddington to Swansea, while 1017 WESTERN WARRIOR has arrived with 1F41, 15:35 Bristol–Cardiff. No.1034 had been fitted with air-brakes and out-shopped from Swindon Works during late March 1969 and was at this time allocated to Bristol Bath Road. No.1017 was one of the four class members not to be fitted with air-brakes and at this time was allocated to Laira. Arriving from Swansea some ten minutes later was 1069 on 1A62, 15:25 Swansea to Paddington, while 'Hymek' No.7013 had worked 1O65, 16:35 Cardiff to Portsmouth making room for Brush Type 4 No.1663 to arrive with its stock to form the 17:15, 1M74 to Manchester. In addition to all this activity, freight traffic was rolling through behind local Canton-based English Electric Type 3s (later Class 37). **Photo P. Crawley**

The old and the new order was recorded at Cardiff on Saturday, 16 October 1976. A scruffy No.1058 WESTERN NOBLEMAN has arrived at Cardiff with a rugby special in connection with the International that day at Cardiff Arms Park. Meanwhile, HST 253 010 arrives from Swansea with a Paddington service. The newly introduced HSTs released the Class 47s that had hauled the Paddington to Swansea service, so hastening the end of the 'Westerns'. It was not just Class 50s that took over passenger duties on the 'Western' as the gradual introduction of HSTs also had a direct effect. It was only for a very few months that one could see 'Westerns' and HSTs running alongside each other on the Region. **Photo Stephen C Marshall**

No.1031 WESTERN RIFLEMAN stands at Barry Island having worked a day excursion from Hayes to the resort on Sunday, 7 July 1974. This was not the only 'Western' to visits the resort that day as No.1050 arrived on an excursion from Plymouth. Barry Island was quite a popular destination for excursions in the summer months. This made a change from the local DMU service, one of which is seen about to depart for Cardiff and the valleys alongside 1031. Note the freshly painted maroon patch under the coupling of 1031. Some repairs have obviously been carried out and blue paint must have been in short supply! **Photo T. Wardle**

'Westerns' at Swansea station on Good Friday, 12 April 1974. The view of the top end of the platforms shows Nos.1041 WESTERN PRINCE on the 5Z90, 1630 Swansea to Old Oak Common empty coaching stock and 1064 WESTERN REGENT on 1A73, 16:53 Swansea to Paddington. Prior to October 1971 Landore depot at Swansea had its own allocation of 'Westerns' for the London services. The first air-braked 'Westerns' were based here and were used along with Brush Type 4s on the Swansea to London services. Despite Landore losing its 'Western' allocation, they were still seen working into South Wales to the end. With the advent of electric train heating, the services they could work was restricted but members of the Class continued to appear on selected passenger services, vans and freight traffic. On the 20 January 1977, No.1013 worked the Swansea to Leeds service throughout, the last service train to depart Swansea behind a 'Western'. **Photo T. Wardle**

No.1003 WESTERN PIONEER is pictured on the bridge crossing the River Towy at Carmarthen on Saturday, 3 August 1974 in the early morning light. Booked to arrive at Carmarthen at 0644 and depart at 0727 the locomotive had brought in the 1C87 00:50 Paddington to Milford sleeper, parcels and newspaper service and, following some shunting, is about to continue its journey west to Milford Haven. This bridge no longer carries the railway, the track having been ripped up and no overnight services now serve Milford Haven. Behind 1003 is the station pilot, Class 08 diesel-electric shunter No.08659 with a number of vans and coaching stock. Class 47 No.47070 had worked the train from Paddington to Swansea, 1003 going forward into West Wales and working through to Milford Haven. Those were the days when it was still possible to travel overnight from the capital to West Wales in sleeping car accommodation **Photo T. Wardle**

No.1055 WESTERN ADVOCATE arrives at Llanelli with 1A73, the 14:40 Fishguard to Paddington on Saturday, 6 July 1974. The locomotive had worked into Fishguard on the 07:50 Paddington service. No.1055 had a windscreen wiper motor modification fitted and the yellow box can be clearly seen in this photograph on the driver's side. As ADVOCATE was the only 'Western' to carry this modification it could be easily identified when looking at this end. No.1055 looks rather care-worn having been last out-shopped from Swindon during late December 1970 and not having had a Laira repaint since May 1973. **Photo T. Wardle**

A visit to Carmarthen on a hot weekday August afternoon during 1970 finds 1073 WESTERN BULWARK stabled in the station platforms. Last of the Class, BULWARK was at this time allocated to Landore, Swansea, having been dual-braked and released from Swindon during December 1969 and re-allocated from Laira. No.1073 returned to Laira from May 1971, but was not the most common of 'Westerns' seen in the West Country, perhaps spending more time in West Wales as this picture illustrates. **Photo D. Nicholls**

Having reached the end of the line at Milford Haven, 1003 WESTERN PIONEER backs the empty stock of the sleepers from the 1C87, 00:50 Paddington service into the sidings on Saturday, 3 August 1974. The sleeper was timed to arrive at 08:50 and included passenger coaches from Swansea. From Paddington it was advertised as sleepers only, though in it always included some compartment passenger stock. This was not the only overnight service to reach the town as a 01:10 Bristol Temple Meads to Milford Haven service also ran, arriving at 06:44. Photographs of 'Westerns' working service trains on West Wales lines are relatively rare but this would once have been an everyday scene especially when Landore had its allocation in the 1960s. Trains such as these are now, like the 'Westerns' themselves, long gone and only multiple units work these lines. No.1003 was running on borrowed time as its last day in traffic was 16 September some six weeks later. Note the temporary repair to the side damage around the marker light on the right-hand side. No.1003 had obviously worked 1C51 at some point to Swansea. In the background freight wagons can be seen standing in the yard. **Photo T. Wardle**

On the evening of Friday, 24 October 1975 the Wirral Railway Circle ran the 'Pembroke Coast Express' railtour from Crewe to West Wales. On arrival at Cardiff, No.47555 was removed and No.1013 WESTERN RANGER worked forward with the tour visiting Fishguard Harbour, Milford Haven and Pembroke Dock on Saturday, 25 October. This gave participants the chance to enjoy 'Western' haulage on all the lines in West Wales where the Class had worked in the past. No.1013 is seen here at Whitland carrying two headboards both clearly showing this was the Pembroke Coast Express. Whitland at this time still had a large creamery which despatched milk to the capital and you can see milk tanks stabled in the sidings in the background. The silver buffers on 1013 are showing signs of wear even though the locomotive had been repainted at Laira depot between September 9 and 13 1975. **Photo B.Mills**

The 'Pembroke Coast Express' railtour is seen at Pembroke Dock on Saturday, 25 October 1975, with 1013 WESTERN RANGER having run round and waiting to depart back to Whitland. The sidings on the right do not appear to have seen much recent activity judging by the surface rust on the rails. This is thought to have been the last 'Western' to work out of Pembroke Dock terminus. They were not particularly common at this location, Class 37s or 47s being more regular performers. Prior to this working, No.1057 had worked a Christmas shopping special from Pembroke Dock to Paddington on Saturday, 30 November 1974, departing the station at 05:50. Today the branch line sees only contemporary diesel multiple units. **Photo B. Mills**

No.1068 WESTERN RELIANCE, in a rather weathered state, has brought the 07:50 from Paddington into Fishguard Harbour station on Saturday, 21 July 1973, and is seen shunting the stock into the sidings by the cliff. The reason for this was due to Brush Type 4 No.1610 working a 07:55 1Z33 Paddington-Fishguard Harbour relief which required access to the platforms. No.1068 would later work the 14:35 Fishguard to Paddington service. Other 'Westerns' recorded at work in West Wales that day included No.1000 with the morning empty coaching stock from Milford Haven to Carmarthen, then working the 19:15 Milford Haven-Paddington forward from Carmarthen as far as Swansea. That evening No.1059 worked the 19:50 Swansea-Fishguard Harbour. **Photo T. Wardle**

Despite it being a very gloomy day, the location is unmistakably Chesterfield on Thursday, 20 January 1977 with No.1013 WESTERN RANGER far from home working the 07:30 Swansea to Leeds. Back in Cornwall we learned how 1013 had worked this service from Swansea following the failure of the booked locomotive. As the only boiler-fitted engine on shed at the time, No.1013 was substituted with the expectation that it would be taken off at Gloucester. As events unfolded there was no replacement locomotive either at Gloucester or Birmingham, so unbelievably the 'Western' worked through to Leeds with, I believe, a Gloucester driver and a conductor driver where required. RANGER fuelled at Neville Hill and returned on the 14:43 Leeds-Plymouth. Other than pictures taken at Leeds, this is the only picture I have ever seen of the working en route. Fortunately Chesterfield photographer Peter Crawley had his camera with him to record this historic working. This has to be one of the rarest workings of a 'Western' on a service train and that it took place just weeks before the Class became extinct was even more very remarkable. I wonder what locations 'Westerns' managed to reach unrecorded in the 1960s when few people were interested in photographing diesels? **Photo P. Crawley**

Here is the photographer's tale:

It was partially a matter of luck that I had my camera with me on this memorable occasion as we had not been tipped off! At that time I was working in Chesterfield and virtually every week lunch time I and one or two others used to take our sandwiches down to the Fish Dock at Chesterfield station to watch trains and I always had my camera with me just in case something appeared that needed photographing. It wasn't a state of the art camera, but a Rank Mamiya 35mm (not a SLR). It took reasonably good photographs, even better if the sun was out. My early stuff was taken on this camera with some very good results. Anyway, as we approached the 'Wall' (now sadly fenced off), a friend of ours who was a porter at the station greeted us with the news that there was a 'Western' on the Swansea- Leeds due in around ten minutes. We did not know whether to believe him or not, it seemed such a fantasy. Anyway we were eating our butties and looking south, when around the long curve a Horns Bridge we saw a yellow front approaching - IT WAS A 'WESTERN'! Hardly believing my eyes I took the photo, pity it was such a dull day. We then raced through the car park and dashed by the ticket barrier, down the steps and through the subway to Platform 2. By this time the guard was blowing his whistle and D1013 powered away. The train had only stopped for a minute as it was running a few minutes late. I only managed to get a going away shot - unfortunately I could not get the shot with the crooked spire in the background. The train did not have many people on it and I think that there was just a couple of lucky enthusiasts in the front coach. I went down for the return working, but it was running rather late and I had to return to work (I had sneaked out and dare not be 'missing' any longer). However, I have the only photo of D1013 at Chesterfield on that amazing northbound working – the rarest 'Western' working ever! I later did get a 'Western' with the crooked spire as a backdrop when D1023 worked the 'Western Finale' Exeter-York special a few weeks later, though it was a dull day again. Happy memories!